Programming Concepts in C++

-A Hands-on Approach

V.UMA

Assistant Professor
Dept. of Computer Science
Pondicherry University

ISBN: 9781692942410

DEDICATION

This book is dedicated to my husband, Baskar, and to my children, Hamsika and Nandita.

CONTENTS

PREFACE

Thank you for purchasing this book. This handbook will help you explore, harness, and gain appreciation of the competencies and features of C++. This book contains several examples that would enable you to learn C++ Programming swiftly and commendably.

C++ is a high-level, object oriented programming language. This book provides all essential programming concepts and information you need to start developing your own C++ program. The book not only contains useful and in-depth information on the conceptual foundations of the language but also teaches you how to implement each language concept programmatically. Each chapter is equipped with number of code snippets making it easy for the reader to understand and learn the language fast.

All the examples provided in this book have been executed successfully on CodeLite IDE. You are hereby instructed to implement the code in the same platform for successful execution and better understanding.

1 INTRODUCTION

- C++ is a general-purpose, high level, object oriented programming language.
- It was developed by Bjarne Stroustrup, and released in 1979.
- It works on different platforms (Windows, Mac, Various versions of Unix etc).
- C++ provides a clear understanding about the object oriented programming concepts.
- It is used in developing real time application systems and system software like editor, compiler etc.
- Polymorphism, Data hiding, Inheritance, Early and late binding are some characteristics that C++ holds.
- It follows bottom-up programming approach.
- It provides the benefit of reusability.
- C++ programs are easily maintainable and expandable.

This book first introduces the basic concepts in C++ initially. In the later chapters, the advanced concepts viz. Polymorphism, Inheritance, Virtual functions, File handling, Templates and Exception handling are discussed. The programs given in this book have been implemented and tested on CodeLite IDE. In the example programs, the #include statements and main function declaration are not shown. The reader is expected to include those statements in the program while executing the example programs.

2 KEYWORDS, IDENTIFIERS AND VARIABLES

2.1 KEYWORDS

- ➢ Refer to reserved words which have special meaning.
- ➢ Keyword cannot be used as variable name, function name or identifiers.
- ➢ Keywords are Case sensitive.
- ➢ Table 2.1 lists the C++ keywords.

Table 2.1 *C++ keywords*

asm	double	new	switch
auto	else	operator	template
break	enum	private	this
case	extern	protected	throw
catch	float	public	try
char	for	register	typedef
class	friend	return	union
const	goto	short	unsigned
continue	if	signed	virtual
default	inline	sizeof	void
delete	int	static	volatile
do	long	struct	while

2.2 IDENTIFIERS

➢ Identifiers are names given to entities like class, functions, variables etc.
➢ It helps in differentiating one entity from another.

Rules for identifiers
1. Identifiers can be combination of letters in lowercase(a to z) or uppercase (A to Z) or digits(0 to 9) or an underscore(_).
2. An identifier cannot start with a digit.
3. Keywords cannot be used as identifiers.
4. We cannot use special symbols like !,@,#,$,% etc. as identifiers.
5. Identifiers are case sensitive.

TABLE 2.2 *Examples of identifiers*

IDENTIFIERS	VALIDITY	REMARKS
Num_1=23	Valid	Satisfies rule 1,2,4.
1_num=23	Not valid	Does not satisfy rule 2.
Num_1_mark=45	Valid	Satisfies rule 1,2,4.
enum=2	Not valid	Does not satisfy rule 3.
mark@= 23	Not valid	Does not satisfy rule 4.

2.3 COMMENTS

➢ Comments are ignored by compilers or interpreters.
➢ It makes code more readable.
➢ // symbol is used to write the comment.

TABLE 2.3 *Examples of comments*

SYMBOL	PURPOSE	EXAMPLE
//	Single line comment	//test statement
/* */	Multiline comments	/* This is a sample program for Calculating the simple interest */

2.4 CONSTANTS

➢ Symbolic (Named) constants are defined using the qualifier **const.**
➢ Value declared using **const** cannot be modified in the program.
➢ **Enum** keyword is used to define a set of integer constants.

TABLE 2.4 *Examples of constants*

SYNTAX	PURPOSE
const int num=10;	Declare a named constant num of type int.
const num=10;	Declare a named constant num of type int.
extern const num=10;	Declare a named constant num of type

	int that can be referenced from another file.
enum {A, B, C};	Define integer constants A, B and C with values 0,1 and 2 respectively.
enum {A=50, B=20, C=10};	Define integer constants A, B and C with values 50,20 and 10 respectively.

2.5 EXPRESSIONS

➢ Combination of operators, constants and variables.
➢ Can be function calls with return values.

TABLE 2.5 *Types of Expressions*

TYPE	SYNTAX	REMARKS
Constant expression	10	Constant values.
Integer expression	a * b /10	Produces integer results with a and b being integer variables.
Float expression	x / y	Produces floating point results with x and y being float variables.
Pointer expressions	ptr*2	Produces address values with ptr being a pointer variable.
Relational	a + b > 50	Produces a value **True** or

expressions		**False.**
Logical expressions	a > b && b > c	Produces a value **True** or **False.**
Bitwise expressions	a << 2	Produces a value by shifting bits to the left.
Chained assignment	a=b=10	10 is assigned to b and a.
Embedded assignment	a= (b=5) + 10	b will be assigned 5 and a will be assigned 15.
Compound assignment	a+=5	5 will be added to the existing value of variable a and will be assigned back to a.

2.6 VARIABLES

- ➢ Variable is a location in memory used to store some data(value).
- ➢ They are given unique names.
- ➢ Rules for mentioning variable name are same as identifiers.
- ➢ In C++, the variables are to be declared before using it.
- ➢ Variable name can have maximum 31 characters.
- ➢ Variable type can be char, int, float, double, void, wchar_t and bool.

TABLE 2.6 *Examples of variable assignment*

TYPES OF ASSIGNMENT	EXAMPLES	REMARKS

Single assignment	int num=10;
	
	float height=5.5;
	
	char name[10]="raj";
	
	char sex='f';
		integer, float, character type variables being initialised.

Multiple assignment	int num1=num2=10;	Error.

Dynamic initialisation	int num1=10;
	
	int num2=num1/5;
		Variable num2 is initialised dynamically to 2.

Reference variable	int total=10;
	
	int &sum=total;
	
	cout<<sum;
		Variable sum is a reference variable and refers to same data object(total) in memory and the output will be 10.

3 DATATYPES

3.1 INTRODUCTION

- ➤ C++ compilers support all basic data types.
- ➤ Every value in C++ has a datatype.

3.2 BASIC BUILT-IN DATATYPES

- ➤ int
- ➤ char
- ➤ void
- ➤ float
- ➤ double
- ➤ bool

3.2.1 int

- ➤ Integers fall under this category. They are defined as int.
- ➤ unsigned int, signed int, short int, unsigned short int, signed short int, long int, signed long int, unsigned long int are the various modifiers of int data type. They differ in the size and ranges.

Example 3.1

int num=100;

//variable num is of integer data type with value=100

int arr[10];

// variable arr is an array of integer data type

3.2.2 char

- ➤ Used to represent characters.

- ➢ Array of characters is used to represent string.
- ➢ unsigned char and signed char represent different ranges.
- ➢ wchar-t describes wide character.

Example 3.2

char sex='M';

//variable sex is of character data type with 'M' as its value

char name[20]="Raj";

// variable name is a string with Raj as its value

3.2.3 void

- ➢ Used to specify the return type of a function when it is not returning any value.
- ➢ To represent empty argument list of a function.
- ➢ Used in the declaration of generic pointers.

Example 3.3

void func_add(void);

//Function func_add returns nothing and has no arguments

Example 3.4

void *ptr1;   // ptr1 is a generic pointer

int *ptr2;   // ptr2 is an integer pointer

ptr1=ptr2;   //int pointer is assigned to void pointer

3.2.4 float

- ➢ Used to represent floating point number.

Example 3.5

float num=10.5;
//variable num is of float data type with value=10.5

float arr[10];   // variable arr is an array of float data type

3.2.5 double

> Used to represent floating point number with more precision.
> Modifier long double is used to represent floating point numbers of large size and range.

Example 3.6

double num=1000001.5345;
//variable num is of double data type

3.2.6 bool

> Represents truth values-True/False.

Example 3.7

bool pass= true;
//variable pass is of boolean data type
bool pass=false;

3.3 USER DEFINED DATATYPES

3.3.1 STRUCTURE

> Holds variables of different data types.
> The variables declared in a structure are called as structure members or elements.
> Structures are defined using **struct** keyword.
> The structure members can be accessed using dot or period operator.

- Structure members can be declared using private members and hence can preserve data hiding.
- Structure name can be used to create variables of the structure.
- Structures can hold data and functions.
- Since **class** holds both data and functions, structures are used for holding only data.

Example 3.8

Program

```
struct student

{

int x, y;                //x, y are public members

float num1, num2;    // num1,num2 are public members

};

void main()

{

student s1;

s1.x=100;

s1.num1=23.25;

cout<<s1.x<<"\n";

cout<<s1.num1;

}
```

Output

100

23.25

Example 3.9

```
struct student
{
private:
  int x, y;                    // x,y are private members
public:
  float num1, num2;    // num1, num2 are public members
};
void main()
{
  student s1;              //creating variable of structure
  //s1.x=100;Error x is not accessible as it is a private variable
  s1.num1=23.25;
  //cout<<s1.x; Error
cout<<s1.num1;
}
```

Output

23.25

3.3.2 UNION

- ➢ Declaration and initialisation starts with union keyword.
- ➢ Structure allocates different memory locations to its members whereas, Union reserves memory corresponding to largest member of the union.

Example 3.10

Program

```
union student
{
int x, y;
float num1, num2;
};
struct course
{
int a,b;
float id1,id2;
};
void main()
{
student s1;
course c1;
```

```
cout<<sizeof(s1)<<"\n";

//memory occupied by union will be given as output

cout<<sizeof(c1);

// memory occupied by structure will be given as output

}
```

Output

4   //size is equal to memory of float variable

12   // size = size of 2 int var+2 float var

3.3.3 CLASS

➢ Class binds data and functions together.
➢ This data type is discussed in detail later in chapter 9.

3.3.4 ENUMERATION

➢ Similar to symbolic constants, enumeration is used to attach names to numbers, improving the readability of the code.
➢ Values 0,1,2 etc. are assigned to the words.
➢ In the example 3.11, fruits become a new type name for which new variables can be declared. For instance,
           fruits guava;
➢ Can be used along with **switch** statement as shown in example 3.12.

Example 3.11

Program

void main()

```
{
enum fruits{apple, orange, grapes};
cout<<apple;
}
```

Output

0   // Apple will be assigned 0

TABLE 3.1 *Examples of enumeration statements*

EXAMPLE STATEMENTS	REMARKS
enum fruits{apple,orange, grapes}; fruits sweet=apple; cout<<sweet;	Output is 0 as sweet will be assigned value of apple which is 0.
enum fruits{apple,orange, grapes}; fruits sweet=0; cout<<sweet;	Error. Integer values cannot be assigned directly to enum variables.
enum fruits{apple,orange=5, grapes=8}; cout<<grapes<<orange;	Output: 8 and 5
enum fruits{apple=4,orange, grapes}; cout<< orange << grapes;	Output: 5 and 6
enum{apple,orange, grapes}; cout<< orange << grapes;	Output: 1 and 2

Example 3.12

Program

```
int main()
{
enum fruits{apple,orange, grapes};
switch(1)
{
case apple:
   cout<<"apple";
   break;
case orange:
   cout<<"orange";
   break;
default:
   cout<<"grapes";
   break;
}
}
```

Output

```
orange    // as value of expression in switch is 1
```

3.4 DERIVED DATATYPES

3.4.1 ARRAY

➢ Array is a collection of data that holds fixed number of values of same type.
➢ Size and type of array cannot be changed after its declaration.
➢ Elements of an array can be accessed using indices.
➢ Array can be initialised.

Example 3.13

```
int marks[5];        //declares an integer array

float price[5];   //declares float array

char name[5];     // declares a character array

cout<< marks[1];  //prints the second element in the array

int marks[5]={20, 12, 34, 45, 56};   //array is initialised

int marks[]={20, 12, 34, 45, 56};   //array is initialised

int num[10][5];    //declares two dimensional array
```

3.4.2 FUNCTION

- ➢ Functions are used to achieve modularity.
- ➢ Functions are discussed in detail in Chapter 8.

3.4.3 POINTER

- ➢ Pointers are symbolic representation of addresses.
- ➢ Address of a variable can be assigned to a pointer variable using & operator.
- ➢ Value stored in an address can be accessed using * operator.
- ➢ Arithmetic operations can be performed on pointers as shown in Table 3.2.
- ➢ Object Pointers are discussed in chapter 12.

Syntax:

Datatype *var_name;

Example 3.14

```
int *ptr;        // ptr points to an address that holds integer data
```

TABLE 3.2 *Statement, output, explanations of pointer operations*

STATEMENT	OUTPUT	EXPLANATION
int *ptr; cout<< ptr <<"\n"; ptr++; cout << ptr;	0x8f8f03f2 0x8f8f03f4	prints address that ptr points to. increments the address value and prints the address.
int *ptr; cout<< ptr <"\n"; ptr--; cout << ptr;	0x8f8f03f2 0x8f8f03f0	prints address that ptr points to. decrements the address value and prints the address.
int *ptr; cout<< ptr <<"\n"; ptr=ptr+4; cout << ptr;	0x8f8f03f2 0x8f8f03fa	prints address that ptr points to. integer (4) is added to the address value and prints the address.
int *ptr1, *ptr2; cout<< ptr1	0x8f920faa	prints address that ptr1 points to.

`<<"\n";`
 	
`cout<< ptr2 << "\n";`
 	
`cout << ptr1-ptr2;`
	0x8f920000
	
	2005
		prints address that ptr2 points to.
		
		prints the difference in address values of ptr1 and ptr2.

`int *ptr1, x=5;`
 	
`ptr1=&x;`
 	
`cout << *ptr1;`
	5	ptr1 is made to point to address of x using & operator.
		
		Content in the address is printed using * operator.

`char *ptr1="Good Morning";`
 	
`cout << ptr1[3];`
 	
`cout<< *(ptr1+3);`
	d
	
	d
		Prints the character at 4th position.

`int *ptr=NULL;`	-	declare a Null pointer.
`int *ptr[10];`	-	Array of pointers.

3.4.4 REFERENCE

> Variable declared as reference is an alternative name for existing variable.
> & operator is used to declare a reference variable.

Example 3.15

Program

```
void main()
{
int x=20;
int& ref_var= x;
//ref_var is a reference variable and is alternative to x
cout<<x<<"\n";
cout<<ref_var<<"\n";
}
```

Output

20

20

3.5 STRING

- ➢ Sequence of Unicode characters (letters, numbers, and special characters).
- ➢ C++ provides new class called **string.**
- ➢ string is a **class which defines objects** that can be represented as stream of characters.
- ➢ Double quotes are used to represent strings.
- ➢ Strings can be indexed.
- ➢ **string** class includes constructors, member functions and operators.
- ➢ **<string.h>** is to be included in the program.

Table 3.3 shows the constructors used to create string objects.

TABLE 3.3 *Statement, output, explanations of basic string constructors*

STATEMENT	EXPLANATION
string str1;	Default constructor that creates an empty or null string object.
string str1 ("apple");	Constructor that initialises the string object.
string str1 ="apple";	Constructor that initialises the string object.
string str1 ("apple"); string str2(str1);	Copy constructor that initialises the string object.
string str1 ("apple"); string str2=str1;	Copy constructor that initialises the string object.

3.5.1 CONCATENATION

Example 3.16

Program

```
string name1="Raj";

string name2="kumar";

cout<<name1+name2;
```

Output

```
Rajkumar
```

3.5.2 LENGTH

Example 3.17

Program

```
string name1="Raj";

cout<<name1.length()<<"\n";

cout<<name1.size();

//both the functions return the length of the string
```

Output

```
3

3
```

3.5.3 STRING COMPARISON

Example 3.18

Program

```
string name1="Raj";

string name2="Raj";

if (name1==name2)

//compares 2 strings and returns 1 if equal

    cout<<"strings are equal";
```

Output

```
strings are equal
```

Example 3.19

Program

```
string name1="Raj";

string name2="Raj";

int val=name1.compare(name2);

//compares 2 strings and returns 0 if equal

if(val==0)      //returns value  >0 if string2 is greater than
//string1 and <0 otherwise

    cout<<"strings are equal";
```

Output

strings are equal

3.5.4 SUBSCRIPTING THE STRING

Example 3.20

Program

```
string name1="Raj";

cout<<name1[2];
```

Output

J

3.5.5 SEARCHING FOR A SUBSTRING

Example 3.21

Program

```
string name1="Rajkumar";

cout<<name1.find("a")<<"\n";

 //return the index of first occurrence of 'a'

cout<<name1.find_first_of("a")<<"\n";

//returns the index of first occurrence of 'a'

cout<<name1.find_last_of("a");

//returns the index of last occurrence of 'a'
```

Output

1

1

6

3.5.6 INSERTING A SUBSTRING

Example 3.22

Program

```
string name1="Raj";

cout<<name1.insert(2,"mra");   //inserts at 3rd position
```

Output

Ramraj

3.5.7 STRING REPLACEMENT

Example 3.23 shows the initialisation of 2 strings. Table 3.4 shows the results of various statements when executed on the initialised strings.

Example 3.23

Program

> string name1="This is C Program";
>
> string name2="C++ OOP Concepts";

TABLE 3.4 *Statement,output,explanations of various string operations*

STATEMENTS	OUTPUT	EXPLANATION
cout<<name1.replace(8, 1,name2);	This is C++ OOP Concepts Program	Replaces 1 character(i.e.C) at 9th position of the name1 string object with the whole string object(name2).
cout<<name1.replace(8, 1,name2,0,7);	This is C++ OOP Program	Replaces 1 character(i.e. C) at 9th position of the name1 string object with characters (7 characters starting from 1st position) of the name2 string object.

cout<<name1.replace(8, 1,"C++ OOP",3)	This is C++ Program	Replaces 1 character(i.e.C) at 9th position of the name1 string object with the given string. The last parameter specifies the size of the replacing string.

3.5.8 STRING SWAPPING

Example 3.24

Program

```
string name1="Raj";

string name2="kumar";

name1.swap(name2);   //2 strings are swapped

cout<<name1<<"\n";

cout<<name2;
```

Output

```
kumar

Raj
```

3.5.9 ERASING THE STRING

Example 3.25

Program

string name1="This is C Program";

cout<<name1.erase(8,2);

//erases 2 characters starting from 9th position

Output

This is Program

3.5.10 DISPLAYING THE SUBSTRING

Example 3.26

Program

string name1="Hello World";

cout<<name1.substr(3,2);

//returns the substring of length 2 starting from index 3

Output

lo

Other string operators are !=(Inequality), <(less than), >(greater than), >=(greater than or equal to) and <=(less than or equal to).

4 INPUT AND OUTPUT OPERATIONS

➢ cin and cout with >> and << operators are used for input and output operations respectively.

➢ The header file to be included in the program is **iostream.**

➢ **put()** is used along with cout to output a line of text, character by character.

> **Syntax: cout.put(char);**

➢ **get()** is used along with cin to get single character as input.

> **Syntax: cin.get(char);**

➢ **getline()** used with cin function reads a whole line of text that ends with a newline character.

> **Syntax: cin.getline(line, size);**

➢ **write()** used with cout function writes a whole line of text that ends with a newline character.

> **Syntax: cout.write(line, size);**

4.1 OUTPUT OPERATIONS

Syntax

> cout<<item1<<item2<<......<<itemN;

Examples (include string.h in the program)

1. cout<<"hello world";   //output: "hello world"

2. char a[20]="how are you";

   cout<<"hai "<<a;   //output: hai how are you

3. int a=2019;

   cout<<"happy new year "<<a;   //output: happy new year 2019

4. char a[6]="hai ", b[10]="welcome";

   cout<<a<<b;   //output: hai welcome

5. int a=10, b=10;

   cout<<a+b;   //output: 20

6. char c='x';

   cout.put(c);   //output: x

7. char c[10]="welcome";
   int i=0;
   while(c[i]!='o')
   {
     cout.put(c[i]);
     i++;
   }   // output: welc

8. char c[10]="welcome";
   int i=strlen(c);   // returns the length of the string
   cout.write(c,i);   //output: welcome

4.2 INPUT OPERATIONS

Syntax

              cin>>item1>>item2>>.....>>itemN;

Examples

  1. int num;
     cin>>num; // accepts an integer from the keyboard

2. char sex;;

   cin>>sex;   //accepts a character from the keyboard

3. char sex;

   cin.get(sex); //accepts a character from keyboard

4. char name[20];

   cin.getline(name,20);

   //accepts characters from keyboard until new line is
   //encountered or the size specified is reached

4.3 FORMATTED I/O OPERATIONS

Formatted output operations can be performed using any of the following methods.

➢ Using **ios** format functions
➢ Using Manipulators

4.3.1 ios FORMAT FUNCTIONS

Table 4.1 explains the most important ios format functions and their usage using suitable examples.

Table 4.1 *Statement,output,explanations of various ios format functions*

FUNCTIONS	STATEMENTS	OUTPUT & EXPLANATION
width()	cout.width(30); cout<<name;	output will be printed in a field of width 30 characters and at right end of the field.

precision()	float num=23.3456;
	
	cout.precision(4);
	
	cout<<num;
		output: 23.34
		
		4 digits will be printed.

30

fill()	int num=23;
	
	cout.fill('*');
	
	cout.width(8);
	
	cout<<num;
		output: *****23
		
		In a field width of 8, the value of num will be printed(right justified) and the empty spaces will be filled with "*".

setf()	float num=23.34567;
	
	cout.setf(ios::scientific, ios::floatfield);
	
	cout<<num;
		output: 2.334567e+001
		
		outputs the value in scientific notation.

setf()	float num=23.34567;
	
	cout.width(20);
	
	cout.setf(ios::showpoint);
	
	cout<<num;
		output:23.34567 displayed right justified in a width of 20 with remaining spaces filled with spaces.

4.3.2 MANIPULATORS

Iomanip header file is to be included in the program.

Syntax

> **cout<<manip1<<manip2<<item;**

More than 1 manipulator functions can be combined. Table 4.2 explains the most important manipulator functions and their usage using suitable examples.

Table 4.2 *Statement,output,explanations of various manipulator functions*

FUNCTIONS	STATEMENTS	EXPLANATION

setw()	float num=23;
	
	cout<<setw(20)<<num;
		Works very similar to width() ios function explained in Table 4.1.

setprecision()	float num=23.3456;
	
	cout<<setprecision(4)<<num;
		Works very similar to precision() ios function explained in Table 4.1.

setfill()	float num=23.34567;
	
	cout<<setw(20)<<setfill('*')<<num;
		Works very similar to fill() ios function explained in Table 4.1.

setiosflags()	float num=23.34567;
	
	cout<<setiosflags(ios::scientific)<<num;
		Works very similar to setf() ios function explained in Table 4.1.

endl	float num=23.34567; cout<<num<<endl; cout<<"end";	Inserts newline after printing the value in num variable.

5 OPERATORS

Operators are special symbols that are used in performing computations.

Various types of operators are

1. Arithmetic operators
2. Relational operators
3. Boolean operators
4. Bitwise operators
5. Assignment operators
6. Special operators

5.1 ARITHMETIC OPERATORS

Various arithmetic operators are   +(Addition),-(Subtraction), *(Multiplication), /(Division), and %(Modulo Division)

Example 5.1 shows the initialisation of 2 integer variables. Table 5.1 shows the results of various arithmetic operations executed on the variables.

Example 5.1
Program

        int a,b;

        a=10;

        b=20;

TABLE 5.1 *Statement, output and explanation of various arithmetic operations*

STATEMENT	OUTPUT	EXPLANATION
cout<<(a+b);	30	Addition operation

cout<<(a-b);	-10	Subtraction operation
cout<< (a*b);	200	Multiplication operation
cout<< (a/b);	0	Division operation
cout<< (a%b);	10	Mod operation

5.2 RELATIONAL OPERATORS

<, >, ==, !=, >=, <= are comparison(relational) operators.

Example 5.2 shows the initialisation of 2 variables. Table 5.2 shows the results of various relational operations executed on the variables.

Example 5.2

Program

```
int a,b;

a=10;

b=20;
```

TABLE 5.2 *Statement, output and explanation of various relational operations*

STATEMENT	OUTPUT	EXPLANATION
cout<< (a<b);	1	Less than operation
cout<< (a>b);	0	Greater than operation
cout<< (a==b);	0	Equal to operation

5.3 LOGICAL OPERATORS

&&, | | and ! are logical operators.

Example 5.3

Program

```
void main()

{

int a,b;

a=10;

b=20;

if((a>10) && (b>20))    //checks if both conditions are True

  cout<<"True";

else

  cout<<"False";

}
```

Output

```
False
```

5.4 BITWISE OPERATORS

Bitwise operators are &(AND) , |(OR), ~(NOT), ^(XOR), >>(Right shift) and <<(Left shift).

Example 5.4

Program

```
int a,b;

a=10;

b=5;

cout<<(a & b)<<"\n";        # bitwise AND operations

cout<<(a | b);        #bitwise OR operation
```

Output

```
0

15
```

5.5 ASSIGNMENT OPERATORS

Various assignment operators are =, +=, -=, *=, /= and %=

Example 5.5

Program

```
a=10;

a+=10;        //add and assignment operations

cout<<(a);
```

Output

```
20
```

Similarly we can perform various operations using other assignment operators.

5.6 SPECIAL OPERATORS

5.6.1 SCOPE RESOLUTION OPERATOR

> ➤ :: is scope resolution operator.
> ➤ Used to access global variable from an inner block

Example 5.6

Program

```
int a=10;

void main()

{

int a=20;

cout<<a<<"\n";   // accesses the local variable a

cout<<::a;       // accesses the global variable a

}
```

Output

```
20

10
```

5.6.2 DELETE OPERATOR

> ➤ Used to free memory space by destroying the object.

Example 5.7

Program

int *ptr;

delete ptr; //releases the memory space

5.6.3 NEW OPERATOR

➤ Used to allocate memory space by creating an object.

Example 5.8

Program

int *ptr;

ptr=new int; //allocates the memory space

5.6.4 MEMBER DEREFERENCING OPERATORS

➤ ::* is used to declare a pointer to member of a class.
➤ * is used access a member using object name and pointer to that member.
➤ ->* is used to access a member using a pointer to the object and a pointer to that member.

5.6.5 MEMORY MANAGEMENT OPERATORS

➤ malloc() and calloc() functions are used to allocate memory dynamically.
➤ free() function is used to free the allocated memory.
➤ sizeof() operator computes the size of the data object.

6 DECISION MAKING AND BRANCHING

6.1 IF STATEMENT AND ITS VARIANTS

- ➤ If, else if, else statements are conditional statements.
- ➤ They are used in decision making.

Example 6.1

Program

```
void main()

{

int num=17;

if(num%2 == 0)

   cout<<"Even Number";

else

   cout<<"Odd Number";

}
```

Output

Odd Number

Example 6.2

Program

```
void main()
```

```
{
int num=17;
if(num%2 == 0)
    cout<<"Even Number";
else if(num%2 == 1)
    cout<<"Odd Number";
}
```

Output

Odd Number

Example 6.3:

Program

```
void main()
{
int num1=14;
int num2=17;
if((num1%2 == 0)&&(num2%2==0))
    cout<<"Both are Even Numbers";
else if((num1%2 == 1)&&(num2%2==0))
    {
    cout<<"First number is Odd Number\n";
```

```
cout<<"Second number is Even Number";
}
else if((num1%2==1)&&(num2%2==1))
cout<<"Both are Odd Numbers";
else
{
cout<<"First number is Even Number\n";
cout<<"Second Number is Odd Number";
}
}
```

Output

First number is Even Number

Second Number is Odd Number

Example 6.4 Nested if

Program

```
void main()
{
int num1=14;
int num2=18;
if(num1%2 == 0)
```

```
if (num2%2==0)

    cout<<"Both are Even Numbers";

}
```

Output

Both are Even Numbers

Note: 0 and None are considered as false. Everything else is considered as True.

6.2 SWITCH STATEMENTS

> ➤ Multiple branching statement.
> ➤ Expression inside a switch statement should result in constant value.
> ➤ Duplicate case values are not allowed.
> ➤ Default statement is optional.
> ➤ Nested switch is allowed but this reduces the understandability.
> ➤ Break is optional but omission of break statement will result in change of flow of control.

Example 6.5

Program

```
void main()

{

int num1=14, res;

res=num1%2;

switch(res)
```

```cpp
{
case 0: cout<<"Even Number";

        break;

case 1: cout<<"Odd Number";

        break;

default: cout<<"enter valid number";

}

}
```

Output:

Even Number

7 DECISION MAKING AND LOOPING

While, *Do-While* and *for* are looping statements in C++.

7.1 WHILE STATEMENT

➤ Repeats a statement or group of statements if a given condition in the expression is true.
➤ While loop is an Entry controlled loop.

Syntax

```
while (expression)
{
        body of while
}
```

Example 7.1
Program

```
void main()
{
int num=5, i=0;
while (i<num)
{
cout<<i<<"\n";
i=i+1;
}
}
```

Output

```
0
1
2
3
4
```

7.2 DO WHILE STATEMENT

➢ Repeats a statement or group of statements till the given condition in the expression remains true.
➢ Do-While is an Exit controlled loop.

Syntax

```
do
{
body of while
 } while (expression);
```

Example 7.2
Program

```
void main()
{
int num=5, i=0;
do
{
cout<<i<<"\n";
i=i+1;
}while(i<num);
}
```

Output

```
0
1
2
3
4
```

7.3 FOR STATEMENT

➢ Used to execute a set of statements repeatedly.
➢ Initialisation statement is executed only once in the beginning.
➢ The test expression is evaluated and when it returns false value

the loop is terminated.

➤ Otherwise, the update statement is executed.

Syntax:

```
for (initialisation statement; testexpression; updatestatement)
{
body of for
}
```

Example 7.3
Program

```
void main()
{
int i;
for(i=0; i<5; i++)
{
cout<<i<<"\n";
}
}
```

Output

```
0
1
2
3
4
```

7.3.1 NESTED FOR STATEMENT

Example 7.4
Program

```
void main()
{
int i,j;
for(i=1;i<3;i++)
```

```
for(j=1;j<3;j++)
{
  cout<< "i value is "<<i<<"\n";
  cout<<"j value is "<<j<<"\n";
}
}
```

Output

i value is 1
j value is 1
i value is 1
j value is 2
i value is 2
j value is 1
i value is 2
j value is 2

7.4 BREAK, CONTINUE STATEMENTS

➢ Break and Continue statements can alter the flow of the looping statements.
➢ Break statements terminates the block and gets the control out of the loop.
➢ Continue statement takes the control to the next iteration of the loop.

Example 7.5

Program

```
void main()
{ int i,j;
  for(i=1;i<3;i++)
    for(j=1;j<3;j++)
    {
      cout<< "i value is "<<i<<"\n";
      if(i==2)  //when i value is 2 control exits the loop
```

```
    break;    //inner for loop
    cout<<"j value is "<<j<<"\n";
    }
  }
}
```

Output

    i value is 1
    j value is 1
    i value is 1
    j value is 2
    i value is 2

Example 7.6
Program

```
    void main()
    { int i,j;
     for(i=1;i<3;i++)
       for(j=1;j<3;j++)
       {
         cout<< "i value is "<<i<<"\n";
         if(i==2)   //when i value is 2 the control continues with
         continue;  //next iteration of the loop
         cout<<"j value is "<<j<<"\n";
       }
    }
```

Output

    i value is 1
    j value is 1
    i value is 1
    j value is 2
    i value is 2
    i value is 2

8 FUNCTIONS

- ➤ Functions consists of group of statements that can perform a specific task.
- ➤ It enables modular programming.
- ➤ It enables the concept of reusability and enhances readability and understandability.
- ➤ Through Parameters (arguments) values are passed to a function.
- ➤ Return statement returns the value from the function.
- ➤ main() function is the starting point of execution of the C++ program.

Syntax

```
int main()
{
Statements
return 0;
}
```

8.1 ELEMENTS OF FUNCTION

8.1.1 FUNCTION PROTOTYPING

- ➤ Helps the compiler know about the functions defined in the program.
- ➤ Type specifies the return type of the function.
- ➤ If return type is void, it denotes that the function returns nothing.

Syntax

type function_name(parameter1,parameter2,..);

//parameters are optional

Examples:

int sum(int a, float b);

float sum(float a, float b);

void sum(float a, int b);

8.1.2 FUNCTION DEFINITION

Syntax

type function_name(parameter1,parameter2,..)

//parameters are optional

{

statements;

}

8.1.3 FUNCTION CALL

Syntax

Function_name(parameters)

> Function call can be made by using either of the 2 methods mentioned below.
>
> 1. Call by value
> 2. Call by reference

8.1.3.1 CALL BY VALUE

Example 8.1

Program

```
int add(int num1,int num2);
int main()
{
cout<<add(5,10);
return 0;
}
int add(int num1,int num2)
{
    return(num1+num2);
```

}

Output

15

CALL BY REFERENCE

Example 8.2

Program

```
int swap(int &x,int &y);    //x and y are reference variables
int main()
{
int num1=5, num2=10;
cout<<"Before swapping \n";
cout<< num1<<"\n";
cout<< num2<<"\n";
swap(num1,num2);
cout<<"After swapping \n";
cout<< num1<<"\n";
cout<< num2;
return 0;
}
int swap(int &x,int &y)
{
   int temp;
   temp=x;
   x=y;
   y=temp;
}
```

Output

Before swapping

5

10

After swapping

51

10

5

Return by reference returns reference to variables. In the following example, the reference variables are returned to the calling function.

Example 8.3
Program

```
int & check_even(int &x,int &y);
int main()
{
int num1=5, num2=10;
check_even(num1,num2)=0;
cout<<num1<<"\n"<<num2;
return 0;
}
int & check_even(int &x,int &y)
{
   if(x%2==0)
   return(x);
   if(y%2==0)
   return(y);
}
```

Output

5

0

8.1.4 ACTUAL AND FORMAL PARAMETERS

> The parameters that are in the function call are actual parameters.

> The parameters that are present in the function definition are formal parameters.

8.1.5 DEFAULT ARGUMENTS

➢ If an argument in the function definition is assigned a default value and if the function call does not pass any value for this argument, the default value will be considered inside the function.

➢ Default arguments must be used after all non-default arguments in the function definition.

Example 8.4

Program

```
int add(int num,int num1=10);  //num1 is default argument
int main()
{
cout<<add(5);
return 0;
}
int add(int num,int num1)
{
    return(num+num1);
}
//default argument value is not passed to the function
```

Output

15

8.1.6 INLINE FUNCTIONS

➢ Inline function is expanded in line when it is invoked.
➢ Function call is replaced with function code.
➢ Saves memory space as it avoids jumping to the function, pushing variables and addresses in the stack and returning to the calling function.

Syntax

```
inline function-name(parameters)
{
```

Function-body

}

> Invoking the function is similar to normal functions.
> If loop, switch, goto statements are present, inline expansion may not work.
> If inline functions are recursive, inline expansion may not work.
> In the presence of static variables, inline expansion may not work.

Example 8.5

Program

```
inline int sum(int num1,int num2);
//sum is an inline function
int main()
{
int x=5, y=10;
cout<<sum(x,y);
return 0;
}
inline int sum(int num1,int num2)
{
    return(num1+num2);
}
```

Output

15

8.1.7 RETURN STATEMENT

Syntax

```
return(expression_list)
```

8.1.8 SCOPE AND LIFE TIME OF VARIABLES

> Variables defined inside the function have local

scope(recognition).

➤ Life time of those variables (period for which the variables reside in the memory) is the period for which the function executes.

Example 8.6
Program

```
int sum;
int array_sum(int[],int);
int main()
{
int arr1[5]={2,4,6,7,8};
sum=array_sum(arr1,5);
cout<<sum;
}
int array_sum(int arr1[],int n)
{
int total=0,i=0;
   for(i=0;i<n;i++)
      total=total+arr1[i];
return total;
}
```

Output
27

In this example total and i are local variables of function array_sum and the scope of the variables is local to the function. Whereas, the variable sum has global scope and can be accessed outside the function. In order to declare a variable as global, we can declare it outside the main() function.

8.2 TYPES OF FUNCTIONS

Functions are of 2 types.

1. Built-in functions

2. User-defined functions

8.2.1 BUILT-IN FUNCTIONS

Some widely used built-in functions are explained below.
- ➤ The mathematical functions can be used in the program after including the header file math.h.
- ➤ The arguments are of type double and return values are also of type double.

1. abs()-returns absolute value of number specified as argument.

Example 8.7
Program
        cout<<abs(-2);
Output
        2

2. ceil()-returns the rounded value of the number specified as argument.

Example 8.8
Program
        cout<<ceil(2.67);
Output
        3

3. cos()-returns cosine value of the number(in radians) specified as argument.

Example 8.9
Program
        cout<<cos(90);
Output
        -0.448074

Similarly sin() and tan() functions can be used.

4. sqrt()-returns square root of the number specified as argument.

Example 8.10

Program

    cout<<sqrt(16);

}

Output

    4

5. pow(arg1,arg2)-returns arg1 raised to power of arg2.

Example 8.11

Program

    cout<<pow(2,4);

Output

    16

6. exp(x)-returns exponential function e^x.

Example 8.12

Program

    cout<<exp(4);

Output

    54.5982

7. floor()-returns the rounded value of the number specified as argument, by rounding it to a value not greater than the number.

Example 8.13

Program

    cout<<floor(9.7);

Output

    9

8. log()-returns the natural logarithm of the number specified as argument.

Example 8.14

Program

    cout<<log(6);

Output

    1.79176

9. log10()-returns the logarithm of the number specified as argument.

Example 8.15

Program

    cout<<log10(6);

Output

    0.778151

8.2.2 USER DEFINED FUNCTIONS

The function written by the user inorder to perform a particular action is called as user defined function. The function definition, function call, arguments and return statements have been already discussed in section 8.1.

8.3 RECURSIVE FUNCTION

If a function calls itself then it is recursive function. Advantages of recursion are

> ➢ Code is concise.
> ➢ Complex tasks can be done by modularisation.

Disadvantages are

> ➢ It is hard to understand and hence debugging is difficult.
> ➢ It is expensive in terms of memory usage.

Following example finds the factorial of a number by performing recursion.

Example 8.16

Program

```
int fact(int);
int main()
{
cout<<fact(5);
}
int fact(int n)
{
   if(n==0)
   return(1);              //Terminating condition
   else
   {
   return(n*fact(n-1));    //Recursive call
   }
}
```

Output

```
120
```

9 CLASSES AND OBJECTS

9.1 INTRODUCTION TO CLASSES

- ➢ Class is an extension of structures in C.
- ➢ It is a user defined data type.
- ➢ Classes enable data hiding.

9.1.1 CLASS DECLARATION

- ➢ Describes the type and scope of its members.
- ➢ Classes are enclosed with braces and terminated by semicolon.
- ➢ Contains declaration of variables and functions.
- ➢ Variables are known as data members.
- ➢ Functions are known as member functions.
- ➢ The variables and functions are specified under various visibility(access) specifiers.
- ➢ The private members are accessible only from within the class.
- ➢ The public members are accessible from outside the class.
- ➢ Default access specifier is private.
- ➢ Member function can call another member function directly.

Syntax

```
class classname
{
private:
        data members;
        member functions;
public:
        data members;
        member functions;
};
```

Example 9.1

Program

```cpp
class student {
private:
int id, mark;              //data members are private
void reg_num()             //private member function
{
   cout<<"Give phone details";
   cin>>phone;
}
public:
 input()                   //public member function
 {
   cout<<"Give the id\n";
   cin>>id;
   cout<<"Give the mark\n";
   cin>>mark;
 }
 display()                 //public member function
 {
   cout<<"Id is   "<<id<<"\n";
   cout<<"Mark is  "<<mark;
 }
};
int main() {
  //Creating object of class student
  student s;
  s.input();      // Public member function can be accessed
  s.display();    // Public member function can be accessed
  //s.id=25; ERROR as the data member is private
  //s.reg_num(); ERROR as member function is private
  return 0;
}
```

Output

Give the id

1

Give the mark

78

Id is   1

Mark is 78

9.2 OBJECT DECLARATION

➢ Class variables are known as objects.

➢ Objects can be declared in two ways.

Syntax

classname object1, object2,…;

OR

class classname

{

private:

data members;

member functions;

public:

data members;

member functions;

}object1,object2,….;

9.3 ACCESSING CLASS MEMBERS

➢ Class members can be accessed using the objects.

➢ Member function can call another member function directly without using objects.

Syntax

Objectname.function_name(arguments);

9.4 DEFINING MEMBER FUNCTIONS

> ➢ Member functions can be defined in either of the following 2 ways.

1. Outside the class definition.

Syntax

```
Return_type classname::Function_name(arguments)
{
Member function statements
}
```

2. Inside the class definition.

Syntax

```
Return_type Function_name(arguments)
{
Member function statements
}
```

The following example shows how member functions can be defined using the above 2 methods.

9.5 NESTED MEMBER FUNCTIONS

Example 9.2

Program

```
class student {
private:
int id, mark;
int phone;
void reg_num()//Member fn. defined inside the class
{
   cout<<"Give phone details\n";
   cin>>phone;
}
public:
```

```cpp
    void input();
    display()
    {
      cout<<"Id is   "<<id<<"\n";
      cout<<"Mark is  "<<mark;
    }
};
void student::input()//Member fn. defined outside the class
    {
      cout<<"Give the id\n";
      cin>>id;
      cout<<"Give the mark\n";
      cin>>mark;
      reg_num();                    //Nested member function
    }
int main() {
    //Creating object of class student
    student s;
    s.input();
    s.display();
    return 0;
}
```

Output

Give the id

1

Give the mark

79

Give phone details

4142

Id is   1

Mark is 79

9.6 STATIC DATA MEMBERS

- Static members are initialised to 0 when the first object of the class is created.
- Only one copy of the member is created. All the objects share the member.
- Accessible only within the class but the lifetime is the entire program.

Syntax

> **static** datatype variable;

9.7 STATIC MEMBER FUNCTION

- Static function can access only static data members.
- Static member function is called using the classname only.

    Syntax

    > classname::function_name;

Example 9.3
Program

```
class student {
private:
static int num_object;          //static data member
public:
  student()
  {
    num_object++;
//for every object created increment occurs
  }
  static void display()          //static member function
  {
    cout<<"num_objects "<<num_object;
//can access only static members
```

```
        }
    };

        int student::num_object;
        int main() {
            //Creating object of class student
            student s1, s2;
            student::display();
            //Static member function called using classname
            return 0;
        }
```

Output

        num_objects 2

9.8 ARRAY OF OBJECTS

Syntax

        classname object_name[n];

For example,

        student s[50];

In the above sentence, 50 objects of the class type student will be created.

9.9 OBJECTS AS FUNCTION ARGUMENTS

➢ Copy of the object is passed as arguments. This is equivalent to call by value discussed in previous chapter.

➢ Address of the object is passed as arguments. This is equivalent to call by reference discussed in previous chapter.

The following example shows the procedure for implementing call by value method.

Example 9.4

Program

```
class student {
private:
int id,mark;
public:
  //default constructor discussed in next chapter
student()
  {
    id=0;
    mark=0;
  }
  student(int m, int n)//parameterised constructor
  {
    id=m;        //s2.id=2
    mark=n;      //s2.mark=90
  }
  void display(student s)     //object as argument
  {
    id=s.id;     //s1.id=s2.id
    mark=s.mark;        //s1.mark=s2.mark
    cout<<"id is  "<<id<<"\n";
    cout<<"mark is  "<<mark<<"\n";
  }
};
int main() {
  //Creating object of class student
  student s1, s2(2,90);
  s1.display(s2);                 //object passed as argument
  return 0;
}
```

Output

```
id is  2
```

mark is 90

9.10 FRIENDLY FUNCTIONS

- ➤ Enables 2 classes to share a function.
- ➤ Friend functions need not be a member of any of the 2 classes.
- ➤ Friend function declaration should be preceded by the keyword **friend.**
- ➤ Friend function inside the class can access the private members of the class.
- ➤ It cannot be called using the objects of the class.
- ➤ It has objects as arguments and the members of the class are accessed using these objects.
- ➤ It can be declared in the public or private part of the class.
- ➤ Objects can be passed as reference also.

Example 9.5
Program

```
        class teacher;          //Forward declaration of class
        class student {
        private:
        int id,mark;
        public:
          void input()
          {
            cout<<"Give id \n";
            cin>> id;
            cout<<"Give mark \n";
            cin>>mark;
          }
        friend void display(student,teacher);
        //Friend function declaration
        };
```

```cpp
class teacher {
private:
int course_id;
public:
  void teacher_input()
  {
    cout<<"Give course id  \n";
    cin>> course_id;
  }
friend void display(student,teacher);
//friend function declaration
};
  void display(student s,teacher t)
  //friend function definition
  {
    cout<<"id is  "<<s.id<<"\n";
    cout<<"mark is  "<<s.mark<<"\n";
    cout<<"course_id  "<<t.course_id;
  }
int main() {
    student s1;
    teacher t1;
    s1.input();
    t1.teacher_input();
    display(s1,t1);                    //friend function call
    return 0;
}
```

Output

Give id

1

Give mark

70

Give course id

69

235
id is 1
mark is 70
course_id 235

9.11 RETURNING OBJECTS

A function can return objects also.

Syntax

> **return** (object_name);

10 CONSTRUCTORS AND DESTRUCTORS

➢ Constructor enables an object to initialise itself when created.
➢ Destructor enables destroying the objects when they are no longer needed.

10.1 CONSTRUCTOR

➢ Name of the constructor is same as class name.
➢ Constructor should be declared in the public section of the class.
➢ They cannot return values.
➢ They cannot be inherited.
➢ They can have default arguments.
➢ They cannot be virtual.
➢ They make implicit calls to **new** and **delete** when objects are created and destroyed.
➢ Different types of constructor are: Default constructor, Parameterized constructor and Copy constructor.
➢ For example if the class name is student, syntax for declaring a default constructor is

Syntax

```
class student
{
Declaring the data members
public:
student(void);      //Constructor declared
};
student::student(void)  //defining the constructor
{
Initialising data members
}
```

➢ When the object is created the constructor will be invoked automatically.

10.1.1 DEFAULT CONSTRUCTOR

> Constructor with no parameter is called the default constructor.

Example 10.1

Program

```
class student
{
int id, mark;
public:
student(void);      //Default Constructor declared
display(void);
};
student::student(void)  //defining the default constructor
{
id=20;
mark=56;
}
student::display(void)
{
cout<<"id is "<<id<<"\n";
cout<<"mark is "<<mark;
}
int main()
{
        student s;
        s.display();
}
```

Output

id is 20

mark is 56

10.1.2 PARAMETERIZED CONSTRUCTOR

➢ Constructor with parameter(s)/arguments is called the default constructor.

Example 10.2

Program

```
class student
{
int id, mark;
public:
    //Parameterized Constructor declared
        student(int,int);
        display(void);
};
student::student(int m, int n)
//defining the parameterized constructor
{
        id=m;
        mark=n;
}
student::display(void)
{
        cout<<"id is "<<id<<"\n";
        cout<<"mark is "<<mark;
}
int main()
{
        student s(20,56);                          //implicit call
    // student s=student(20,56); Explicit call can also be used
        s.display();
}
```

Output

```
id is 20
mark is 56
```

10.1.3 COPY CONSTRUCTOR

> Used to initialize an object from another object.
> It takes reference to an object of the same class as an argument.

Example 10.3

Program

```
class student
{
int id, mark;

public:
//Parameterized Constructor declared
student(int,int);
student(student&);  //Copy constructor declared
display(void);
};
student::student(int m, int n)
//defining the parameterized constructor
{
    id=m;
    mark=n;
}
student::student(student & st)
//defining the copy constructor
{
    id=st.id;
    mark=st.mark;
}
student::display(void)
{
    cout<<"id is "<<id<<"\n";
    cout<<"mark is "<<mark<<"\n";
}
```

```
int main()
    {
    student s1(20,56);
    s1.display();
    student s2(s1);
    s2.display();
    }
```
Output
    id is 20
    mark is 56
    id is 20
    mark is 56

10.1.4 MULTIPLE CONSTRUCTORS IN A CLASS

➢ Multiple constructors can be included in a single program.

Example 10.4

Program

```
class student
{
int id, mark;
public:
    student()          // default constructor defined
    {
      id=10;
      mark=90;
    }
//Parameterized Constructor defined
    student(int m,int n)
    {
    id=m;
    mark=n;
     }
    student(student & st)
```

```cpp
//Copy Constructor defined
    {
    id=st.id;
    mark=st.mark;
    }
    display()
    {
      cout<<"id is "<<id<<"\n";
      cout<<"mark is "<<mark<<"\n";
    }
};
int main()
{
    student s;
    cout<<"Output of default constructor is\n";
    s.display();
    student s1(20,56);
    cout<<"Output of parameterised constructor is\n";
    s1.display();
    student s2(s1);
    cout<<"Output of copy constructor is\n";
    s2.display();
}
```

Output

Output of default constructor is
id is 10
mark is 90
Output of parameterised constructor is
id is 20
mark is 56
Output of copy constructor is
id is 20
mark is 56

10.1.5 DYNAMIC INITIALISATION OF CONSTRUCTOR

➤ Constructors can be declared and defined using default arguments.

➤ Objects can be dynamically initialised.

Example 10.5

Program

```
class student
{
int id, mark;
public:
student(int m,int n=85)      //n is default argument
    {
    id=m;
    mark=n;
    }
  display()
    {
      cout<<"id is "<<id<<"\n";
      cout<<"mark is "<<mark<<"\n";
    }
};
int main()
{
    int num1;
    cin>>num1;
    student s1(num1);   //dynamic initialisation of constructor
    cout<<"Output of parameterised constructor is\n";
    s1.display();
}
```

Output

```
45                          //given input
Output of parameterised constructor is
```

id is 45

mark is 85

10.2 DESTRUCTORS

➤ Used to destroy objects created using constructor.

➤ Never takes any argument.

➤ Does not return any value.

➤ Will be invoked automatically upon program termination.

➤ **Delete** can be used to free memory space.

Syntax

```
~classname()
{
Statements
}
```

11 INHERITANCE

➢ Supports the concept of reusability.
➢ Mechanism of deriving new (derived) class from existing(base) class.
➢ Different types of inheritance are
   o Single inheritance
   o Multiple inheritance
   o Hierarchical inheritance
   o Multilevel inheritance
   o Hybrid inheritance

Syntax

class derived_classname : visibility_mode base_classname
{
Statements;
}

➢ Visibility mode is optional (Private, Protected or Public). Default mode is Private.
➢ Constructors and destructors cannot be inherited.
➢ Private members cannot be inherited.
➢ Friend functions cannot be inherited.

11.1 SINGLE INHERITANCE

➢ One derived class inherits one base class.

Example 11.1
Program

```
class A {
public:
  display()
  {
    cout<<"Display of class A"<<endl;
```

```
        }
    };
    class B: public A {                    //Class B inherits Class A
    public:
      show()
      {
        cout<<"Show of B class"<<endl;
        display();
      }
    };

    int main() {
      //Creating object of class B
      B obj;
      obj.show();
      return 0;
    }
```

Output

Show of B class

Display of class A

11.2 MULTILEVEL INHERITANCE

➤ One derived class inherits another derived class.

Example 11.2

Program

```
    class A {
    public:
    display()
    {
        cout<<"Display of class A"<<endl;
    }
```

```cpp
};
class B: public A {      //Class B inherits Class A
public:
        show()
        {
        cout<<"Show of B class"<<endl;
        display();
        }
};
class C: public B {                //Class C inherits Class B
public:
        print()
        {
        cout<<"Print of C class"<<endl;
        show();
        }
};

int main() {
        //Creating object of class C
        C obj;
        obj.print();
        return 0;
}
```

Output

    Print of C class
    Show of B class
    Display of class A

11.3 MULTIPLE INHERITANCE

➤ One derived class inherits from more than 1 base class.

Example 11.3

Program

```
class A {
public:
display()
  {
    cout<<"Display of class A"<<endl;
  }
};
class B {
public:
show()
  {
    cout<<"Show of B class"<<endl;

  }
};
class C: public B,public A {
//Class C inherits Class B and Class A
public:
print()
  {
    cout<<"Print of C class"<<endl;
    show();
    display();
  }
};

int main() {
  //Creating object of class C
  C obj;
  obj.print();
  return 0;
}
```

Output

     Print of C class

     Show of B class

     Display of class A

11.4 HIERARCHICAL INHERITANCE

➢ One base class has more than 1 derived class.

Example 11.4

Program

```cpp
class A {
public:
display()
  {
    cout<<"Display of class A"<<endl;
  }
};
class B: public A {          //class B inherits class A
public:
  show()
  {
    cout<<"Show of B class"<<endl;
    display();
  }
};
class C: public A {          //Class C inherits Class A
public:
  print()
  {
    cout<<"Print of C class"<<endl;
    display();
  }
};
```

```
int main() {
  //Creating object of class C
  C obj1;
  obj1.print();
  B obj2;   //creating object of B
  obj2.show();
  return 0;
}
```

Output

```
Print of C class
Display of class A
Show of B class
Display of class A
```

11.5 HYBRID INHERITANCE

➤ Is a combination of more than 1 type of inheritance.

➤ For instance, if multiple and hierarchical inheritance is applied then it results in hybrid inheritance.

➤ The following program shows how hybrid inheritance is achieved using single and multiple inheritance.

Example 11.5

Program

```
class A {
public:
  display()
  {
    cout<<"Display of class A"<<endl;
  }
};
class B: public A {          //Single inheritance
public:
  show()
  {
```

```cpp
        cout<<"Show of B class"<<endl;
        display();
        }

    };
    class C: public B, public A {        //Multiple inheritance
    public:
      print()
       {
         cout<<"Print of C class"<<endl;
         show();
           }
    };

    int main() {
        //Creating object of class C
        C obj1;
        obj1.print();
        B obj2;   //creating object of B
        obj2.show();
        return 0;
    }
```

Output

Print of C class
Show of B class
Display of class A
Show of B class
Display of class A

11.6 VISIBILITY OF MEMBERS

➢ Table 11.1 shows the visibility of the members of base class.

Table 11.1 Visibility of base class members

Base class	Public derived class	Private derived class	Protected Derived class
Private member	Cannot be accessed	Cannot be accessed	Cannot be accessed
Public member	Public members	Private members	Protected members
Protected member	Protected members	Private members	Protected members

12 POLYMORPHISM

➤ Is the ability to take more than 1 form.
➤ Implemented by overloading the functions and operators.
➤ Two types of polymorphism are
  o Compile time polymorphism (early binding, static binding, static linking)
  o Run time polymorphism

12.1 COMPILE TIME POLYMORPHISM

➤ The information of overloading is known to the compiler at the compile time and the compiler selects the appropriate function during compile time itself.
➤ Hence, this is also called as early binding/ static binding/ static linking.
➤ Function overloading and operator overloading supports compile time polymorphism.

12.1.1 FUNCTION OVERLOADING

➤ Same function name is used to create functions that perform a variety of different tasks.
➤ The overloaded functions have different argument lists.
➤ The function prototype having the same number and type of arguments that matches the function call is executed.
➤ If exact match is not found, type conversions (integral promotions, built-in conversions) are performed and a match is found.
➤ When either of the above methods fail, user defined conversions are performed to find a match.

Example 12.1
Program

```cpp
class Calc {
    public:
    int add(int a,int b)          //Function add is overloaded
    {
        return a + b;
    }
    int add(int a, int b, int c)
    {
        return a + b + c;
    }
    int add(char a, float b, int c)
    {
        return a + b + c;
    }
};
int main(void) {
    Calc C;                        //   class object declaration.
    cout<<C.add(10, 20)<<endl;
    //calls the function with argument(int,int)
    cout<<C.add(12, 20, 23)<<endl;
    //calls function with argument(int,int,int)
    cout<<C.add('A',20.4,11);
    //calls function with argument(char,float,int)
    return 0;
}
```

Output

```
30
55
96
```

12.1.2 OPERATOR OVERLOADING

➤ Mechanism of giving special meaning to operators is called operator overloading.

➤ We can overload most of the C++ operators.

➤ Operator that cannot be overloaded are Scope operator (::), Sizeof, member selector(.), member pointer selector(.*) and ternary operator(?:).

➤ The overloaded operator contains atleast one operand of the user-defined data type.

➤ Syntax of the operator cannot be changed. For instance, if + operator is overloaded, it can still be used for addition purpose only.

Syntax

Return_type classname :: **operator** op (arglist)

{

Function statements;

}

➤ Operator functions can be either member functions or friend functions. Table 12.1 gives details about the number of arguments that are to be passed in each case.

Table 12.1 Types of operators and the arguments to be passed to operator function

Types of operator	Member function	Friend function
Unary	No argument	One argument
Binary	One argument	Two arguments

➤ Friend functions cannot be used to overload =(Assignment), ()(Function call), [](Subscripting) and ->(Class member access) operators.

➤ Operator function is to be declared in the public part of the class.

➢ Arguments can be passed either by value or by reference.
➢ Overloaded operators can be invoked using various methods shown in Table 12.2.

Table 12.2 Methods to invoke the operator function

Types of operator	Member function/Friend function
Unary	op x **or** x op
Binary	x op y

Example 12.2
Program
//Program implementing unary operator(++) overloading
//using member function

```
class Incr
{
  private:
    int num;
  public:
    Test()
    {
      num=0;
    }
    void operator ++()      //++ operator overloading
    {
      num = num+2;
    }
    void Print() {
      cout<<"The Count is: "<<num;
    }
};
int main()
```

```
        {
            Incr I;
            ++I;  // calling of a member function "void operator
    ++()"
            I.Print();
            return 0;
        }
```

Output

The Count is: 2

Example 12.3

Program

//Program implementing unary operator(++) overloading
//using friend function

```
        class Incr
        {
          private:
            int num;
          public:
            Test()
            {
                num=0;
            }
            friend void operator++(Incr&);
            void Print() {
                cout<<"The Count is: "<<num;
            }
        };
        void operator ++(Incr& J)      //Friend function
        {
            J.num = J.num+2;
        }
        int main()
```

91

```
    {
        Incr I;
        ++I; // calling of a friend function "void operator ++()"
        I.Print();
        return 0;
    }
```

Output

The Count is: 2

Example 12.4

Program

```
//Program implementing binary operator(+) overloading
//using member function
    class AddString {
    char str1[25];
    public:
        // Parameterized Constructor
        AddString(char s[25])
        {
        // Initialising string
        strcpy(str1,s);
            }
        // Overload Operator+ to concatenate the strings
        void operator+(AddString a)
        {
            cout << "\nConcatenation: " << strcat(str1, a.str1);
        }
    };
    int main()
    {
        // Declaring object
        AddString a1("Welcome ");
        AddString a2("To C++ Programming");
```

```
        // Call operator member function
        a1+a2;
        //concatenation of strings using + operator overloading
        return 0;

    }
```

Output

    Concatenation: Welcome To C++ Programming

Example 12.5
Program
//Program implementing binary operator(+) overloading
//using friend function

```
        class AddString {
        char str1[25];
        public:
            // Parameterized Constructor
            AddString(char s[25])
            {
              // Initialising string
            strcpy(str1,s);
            }
            // Overload Operator+ to concatenate the strings
            friend void operator+(AddString,AddString);
        };
            void operator+(AddString a, AddString b)
            {
                cout << "\nConcatenation: " << strcat(a.str1, b.str1);
            }
        int main()
        {
            // Declaring object
            AddString a1("Welcome");
            AddString a2("To C++ Programming");
```

```
// Call operator friend function
a1+a2;
return 0;
}
```

Output

Concatenation: Welcome To C++ Programming

12.2 RUNTIME POLYMORPHISM

➢ Member function corresponding to the function call is selected during run time.

➢ Run time polymorphism is also known as late binding or dynamic binding.

➢ It is achieved through virtual functions.

To have better understanding of virtual functions, object pointers are discussed in the next section.

12.2.1 OBJECT POINTERS

➢ Pointer can point to an object created by a class.

Example 12.6
Program

```
class student {
private:
int id, mark;        //data members are private
public:
  input()            //public member function
  {
    cout<<"Give the id\n";
    cin>>id;
    cout<<"Give the mark\n";
    cin>>mark;
  }
```

```
    display()              //public member function
    {
  cout<<"Id is  "<<id<<"\n";
  cout<<"Mark is  "<<mark;
    }
};
int main() {
  //Creating object of class student
  student s;
  //creating an object pointer that points to the object s
  student *ptr=&s;
  s.input();
  ptr->display();
//Accessing display() using object pointer
//Above command is equivalent to s.display();
  return 0;
}
```
Output

```
    Give the id
    12
    Give the mark
    90
    Id is   12
    Mark is  90
```

In the above example, ptr is an object pointer and it points to object s. Hence if we use the command s.display() the same output will be produced.It is also seen that object pointers access the member functions using **arrow operator.**

12.2.2 OBJECT POINTERS TO DERIVED CLASS

> ➤ If B is a base class and D is a derived class,
>   ○ B *bptr;   //bptr is pointer to base class

- D *dptr   //dptr is pointer to derived class
- B b;   // b is a base class object
  B *bptr=&b;
//object pointer pointing to base class object
- D d;   // d is a derived class object
  D *dptr=&d;
//object pointer pointing to derived class object

The following program shows how pointers to derived object and virtual function are used to achieve run-time polymorphism.

12.2.3 VIRTUAL FUNCTIONS

Example 12.7
Program

```
class Base
{
public:
    virtual void show() { cout<<" In Base \n"; }
//Virtual function
};

class Derived: public Base
{
public:
    void show() { cout<<"In Derived \n"; }
};

int main(void)
{   Derived d;
    Base *bp = &d;
    bp->show(); // RUN-TIME POLYMORPHISM
    return 0;
```

}

Output

In Derived

In the above example, it is seen that even though pointer bp points to the base class when it is made to point to the derived object, it executes the show() function in derived class. This is because the show() function in base class has been declared virtual. This is how run time polymorphism is achieved in C++.

Rules for virtual functions are

1. The virtual functions should be member of some class.
2. They can be accessed using object pointers.
3. They can be friend of another class.
4. Virtual function in the base class must be defined.
5. Prototype of both functions in base and derived classes should match.
6. Virtual constructors are not allowed whereas, virtual destructors are allowed.
7. They cannot be static members.

A **pure virtual function** is declared by assigning 0 in declaration. The classes which contain pure virtual functions are called as **abstract classes**. They cannot have objects on its own.

If the pure virtual function in base class is not defined in the derived class, the derived class also becomes abstract class.

13 TYPE CONVERSIONS

➢ A type cast is basically a conversion from one type to another. There are two types of type conversion:
   o Implicit type conversion
   o Explicit type conversion

13.1 IMPLICIT TYPE CONVERSION

➢ All the data types of the variables are upgraded to the data type of the variable with largest data type as shown below.
   o bool -> char -> short int -> int ->
   o unsigned int -> long -> unsigned ->
   o long long -> float -> double -> long double

Example 13.1
Program

```
int main()
{
    int a=10;
    char ch='A';
    int c=a+ch;       //character is converted to integer
    cout<<"Result is "<< c;
}
```

Output

Result is 75   //Ascii value of A(65) + 10

13.2 EXPLICIT TYPE CONVERSION

➢ Type casting is done for conversion.
Syntax

type (expression)

Example 13.2

Program

```
int main()
{
    int a=10;
    float b=10.5;
    int c=a+int(b);        //float is converted to integer
    cout<<"Result is "<< c;
}
```

Output

Result is 20

14 FILE HANDLING

➤ Files are used to store the data permanently in non-volatile memory.
➤ **fstream** header file is to be included in the program.
➤ Class **fstream** is used to create input and output stream.

Syntax

fstream filestreamobject;

➤ Class **ofstream** is used to create the output stream.

Syntax

ofstream filestreamobject;

➤ Class **ifstream** is used to create input stream.

Syntax

ifstream filestreamobject;

Various file operations are
1. Opening a file
2. Closing a file
3. Reading from a file
4. Writing to a file

14.1 OPEN A FILE

Files can be opened using two methods.
1. Using constructor
2. Using open()

14.1.1 OPEN A FILE USING CONSTRUCTOR

Syntax
Output mode

ofstream filestreamobject("file name");

Input mode

ifstream filestreamobject("file name");

14.1.2 OPEN A FILE USING OPEN()

Syntax

Output mode

ofstream filestreamobject;

filestreamobject.open("file name",mode);

Input mode

ifstream filestreamobject("file name");

filestreamobject.open("file name",mode);

File can be opened in different modes. Different modes and their description are explained in Table 14.1.

TABLE 14.1 *File opening modes and their descriptions*

PARAMETER	DESCRIPTION
ios::app	Opens file in append mode
ios::ate	Goes to end of the file on opening
ios::binary	Creates a binary file.
ios::in	Opens file for reading only.
ios::out	Opens file for writing only.
ios::trunc	If file exists it truncates the file.
ios::nocreate	If file does not exist, the operation fails.

Files can be opened in different modes as shown below.

ofstream out_file;

out_file.open("example.txt",ios::app)

//opens the file in append mode

14.2 CLOSE A FILE

The command that is used to close the file is

filestreamobject.close()

Sample code   is shown below.

ofstream out_file;

out_file.close()

It is always safe to close the file after reading/writing.

14.3 READ FROM A FILE

- ➢ >>operator is used.
- ➢ Filestreamobject is used to read information from file.

Sample code is given below.

ifstream in_file("SALES.TXT");

in_file>>num;

//information will be stored in num(variable)

14.4 WRITE TO A FILE

- ➢ << operator is used.
- ➢ Filestreamobject is used to write information in the file.

Sample code is given below.

ofstream out_file("SALES.TXT");

out_file<<1234;   //writes 1234 in file

14.5 FILE POINTER MANIPULATION

Various file pointer manipulation operators are

Filestreamobject.seekg();

//moves get pointer to specified position

Filestreamobject.seekp();

//moves put pointer to specified position

Filestreamobject.tellg();

//gives the current position of get pointer

Filestreamobject.tellp();

//gives the current position of put pointer

Sample code is given below.

Filestreamobject.seekg(n);   //positions to nth byte of fileobject

Filestreamobject.seekg(n,ios::cur);

//positions to nth byte of fileobject from current cursor position

Filestreamobject.seekg(n,ios::end);

//positions to n bytes back from end of file

An example program that shows file operations is given below.

Example 14.1

Program

```
int main()
{
    int num;
    ofstream out_file("SALES.TXT");   //open file for output
    out_file<<1234;                    //write to a file
    out_file.close();                  //close a file
    ifstream in_file("SALES.TXT");     //open file for input
    in_file>>num;                      //read from a file
    cout<<"Number is "<<num;
    return 0;
}
```

Output

Number is 1234

14.6 ERROR HANDLING FUNCTIONS

Table 14.2 shows the various error handling functions and their description.

TABLE 14.2 *Error handling functions and their descriptions*

FUNCTION	DESCRIPTION
bad()	Returns true if an invalid operation is attempted.
fail()	Returns true when an input or output operation has failed.
eof()	Returns true if a file open for reading has reached the end.
good()	Return true if no error has occurred.

Sample program showing the usage of eof() function is given below.

Example 14.2

Program

```
int main()
{
    int num;
    ofstream out_file("SALES.TXT");  //opens file for output
    out_file<<1234<<" ";
    out_file<<2345;       //2 values are written in the file
    out_file.close();
    ifstream in_file("SALES.TXT");      //opens file for input
    while(!in_file.eof())  //reads till end of file is reached
    {
    in_file>>num;
    cout<<"Number is "<<num<<"\n";
    }
    return 0;
}
```

Output

```
Number is 1234
Number is 2345
```

15 TEMPLATES

➤ Enables Generic programming as generic classes and functions can be defined.
➤ Templates are otherwise called as parameterized classes or functions.
➤ Templates can also have regular typed parameters.

15.1 CLASS TEMPLATES

Syntax

template<class T>

class classname

{

Class data members and function definition

};

The following example shows how a generic class can be defined to perform integer and float addition.

Example 15.1

Program

```
template <class T>
//T will be substituted with datatype specified while creating
//an object
class Calculator
{
private:
T num1, num2;        //the variables will be of type T
public:
Calculator(T n1, T n2)
{
      num1 = n1;
      num2 = n2;
}
void displayResult()
```

```
        {
        cout << "Numbers are: " << num1 << " and " << num2 <<
        "." << endl;
        cout << "Addition is: " << add() << endl;
        }

        T add()
        { return num1 + num2; }
        };
        int main()
        {
        Calculator<int> intCalc(2, 1);  //T will be integer
        Calculator<float> floatCalc(2.4, 1.2);
        //T will be float
        cout << "Integer Addition results:" << endl;
        intCalc.displayResult();
        cout << endl << "Float addition results:" << endl;
        floatCalc.displayResult();
        return 0;
        }
```

Output

    Integer Addition results:
    Numbers are: 2 and 1
    Addition is: 3
    Float Addition results:
    Numbers are: 2.4 and 1.2
    Addition is: 3.6

Similarly, class templates with multiple parameters can also be defined.

Example 15.2

Program

```
        template <class T1, class T2>   //multiple parameters
        class display
```

```cpp
{
private:
        T1 num1;
        T2 num2;
public:
        display(T1 n1, T2 n2)
        {
                num1 = n1;
                num2 = n2;
        }
        void displayResult()
        {
        cout << "Numbers are: " << num1 << " and " <<
        num2 << "." << endl;
        }
        };
int main()
{
        display<int,float> f1(2, 1.2);
        //parameters are int and float
        display<char,float> f2('A', 1.2);
         //parameters are char and flaot
        cout << "Display results:" << endl;
        f1.displayResult();
        cout << endl << "Display results:" << endl;
        f2.displayResult();
        return 0;

}
```

Output

    Display results:
    Numbers are: 2 and 1.2
    Display results:
    Numbers are: A and 1.2

Syntax:

template<class T>
returntype functionname(arguments of type T)
{
Body of function
};

Example 15.3
Program

```
template <class T>
T FindMax (T a, T b)   //function template
 {
  return (a>b?a:b);
 }
int main ()
 {
 int i=50, j=60, k;
 float l=10.4, m=5.2, n;
 k=FindMax<int>(i,j);
 n=FindMax<float>(l,m);
 cout << k << endl;
 cout << n << endl;
 return 0;
 }
```

Output

60
10.4

Similarly, function templates with multiple parameters can also be defined.

Example 15.4

Program

```
template <class T1, class T2>
//template with multiple parameters
int FindMax (T1 a, T2 b) {
  return (a>b?0:1);
}
int main () {
        int i=50, j=60, k;
        float l=10.4, m=5.2, n;
        k=FindMax<int,float>(i,l);
        //parameters are int and float
        n=FindMax<float,int>(m,j);
        //parameters are float and int
        cout << k << endl;
        cout << n << endl;
        return 0;
}
```

Output

```
0
1
```

➤ template<class T, int n> is also allowed.

15.3 OVERLOADING FUNCTION TEMPLATES

➤ Template functions can be overloaded. Ordinary function with exact match will be executed. In the absence of such a function, template function will be executed.

Example 15.5

Program

```
template <class T1, class T2>
int FindMax (T1 a, T2 b)        //Function template
```

```cpp
{
cout<<"match found in template function\n";
}
int FindMax(int a,int b)          //ordinary function
{
cout<<"match found in ordinary function";
}
int main () {
int i=50, j=60, k;
float l=10.4, m=5.2, n;
FindMax<int,float>(i,l);          //calls function template
FindMax(i,j);                      //calls ordinary function
return 0;
}
```

Output

match found in template function
match found in ordinary function

16 EXCEPTION HANDLING AND DEBUGGING

- ➤ Errors that occur due improper syntax results in syntax error.
- ➤ Errors in programming logic results in logical errors.
- ➤ Errors that can occur at runtime are called exceptions.
- ➤ If exceptions are not handled properly, the program terminates abnormally.
- ➤ Exceptions are of two types namely synchronous and asynchronous exceptions.
- ➤ Out of range index and overflow are synchronous exceptions.
- ➤ Keyboard interrupts are asynchronous exceptions.
- ➤ Code has to be written to hit, throw, catch and handle the exception.

16.1 TRY CATCH STATEMENTS

Syntax

> **try**
> {
> Statements for throwing an exception;
> }
> **catch(type argument)**
> {
> Statements for Handling the exception;
> }
> **catch(type argument)**
> {
> Statements for Handling the exception;
> }

To avoid the exceptions they are to be handled as shown below.

Example 16.1
Program

```
int main()
{
int a=4,b=0;
try
{
  if (b!=0)
     cout<<a/b;
  else
     throw(b);
  //Finds and throws an exception if b value is 0
}
catch(int x)      //exception is caught as argument is integer
{
cout<<("zero division");   //handling the exception
}
}
```

Output

zero division

By writing the exception handling statements the exceptions will be handled properly. In the above example, ZeroDivisionError is handled. More than 1 catch blocks can be present while handling the exceptions.

16.2 CATCH ALL

 ➢ It is optional in C++.
 ➢ It is written at the end of the catch blocks.
 ➢ This block is used to catch all types of exceptions.

Example 16.2
Program

```
int main()
{
```

```cpp
int a=4,b=0;
try
{
  if (b!=0)
      cout<<a/b;
   else
      throw(b);
}
catch(float x)   //executes if the argument passed is float
{
cout<<("float division with zero denominator");

}
catch(...)        //handles all types of exceptions
{
    cout<<"int division with zero denominator";
}
}
```

Output

int division with zero denominator

16.3 NESTED TRY AND CATCH

Try-catch blocks can be nested as shown below.

Example 16.3

Program

```cpp
int main()
{
int a=4,b=0;
try
{
  try
  {
     throw(b);
```

```cpp
        }
    catch(int b)
    {
        cout<<"zero division\n";
        throw;              //re-throwing an exception
    }
    }
    catch(...)
    {
    cout<<("All errors handling");
    }
```

Output

zero division

All errors handling

Some of the standard exceptions in C++ are std::exception, logic_error, runtime_error, bad_alloc, bad_cast, bad_exception and bad_typeid.

17 SUMMARY

This book teaches you the powerful, fast and popular C++ programming language from scratch, assuming that the reader has only basic computer knowledge. This book allows programmers to express ideas, more clearly and to write faster, more efficient code.

By the completion of this book for C++, you will have an in-depth understanding of how to apply advanced programming techniques to achieve your software development needs. Working files are included to allow you to learn using the same files. I hope that this book would have instilled your interest in C++ programming. Keep updating your C++ programming skills and all the best for your bright future.

ABOUT THE AUTHOR

V. Uma, is presently working as Assistant Professor in the Department of Computer Science, Pondicherry University. She received her M.Tech, and PhD degrees in Computer Science from Pondicherry University in 2007 and 2014 respectively. She was awarded the Pondicherry University gold medal for M.Tech. degree in Distributed Computing Systems. She has more than 12 years of teaching experience at Post Graduate level. Her research interest includes Machine Learning, Knowledge representation and reasoning (spatial and temporal knowledge) and Sentiment analysis. She has authored and co-authored more than 20 peer-reviewed journal papers, which includes publications in Springer and Inderscience. She has also authored 3 chapters in various books published by IGI Global. She has received the Best Paper Awards in International Conference on Digital Factory and International Conference on Smart Structures and Systems in the years 2008 and 2019 respectively. She has written a book on Python Programming & Data Analysis-A Beginner's Handbook in 2019.